The Home I
Volume II
How to Make Beer, an Introduction to Home Brewing!

Jeff King

Published by FOI Publishing at
http://www.foipub.com.

Cover photo and Chapter headers: Max Johnson

http://www.TheHomeDistiller.com

The purpose of this workbook is for entertainment and education only.

Please note that while making beer and/or wine in your home is legal under federal law in the United States that may or may not be true of your local regulations. Please consider those before applying anything that you read here.

Also the distillation of alcohol without a license is against the law in the United States of America and many other countries. Please check your federal, state, and local laws prior to following any of the procedures outlined herein.

Contents

Foreword

I came to beer making kind of backwards. My first introduction to brewing started in the back woods of Kentucky. What we were making may have started out a lot like beer but it ended up someplace quite different. You see, I got my start as a moonshiner. It wasn't till many years later when, in an effort to perfect my distilling skills, I decided to go back to the basics and find out how to brewing and beer making really works.

I had moved to the big city and in an effort to find the ingredients I needed I ended up at a local home brew shop. I was like a kid in a candy store. I realized quickly that these guys were very serious about getting everything they could out of their mash. They had concepts and techniques I had never contemplated.

I have a personal belief that if there is anything you want to master the first thing you need to do is to find out how it works, at the nuts and bolts level that is. My father first taught me how to fix a car before he would teach me to drive. I had to learn how to strip and clean my rifle before he taught me how to shoot. But it seems that when it came to brewing, I had missed a step. I had overlooked the first and most crucial part, the art of making beer, but I soon remedied that error. I dove into the study of grains and hops, lagers and ales. Now years later I don't know how I ever got so far without truly understanding the basics.

So whether you are a fellow home distiller looking to expand your skills or just simply new to brewing of any kind this is the book for you. We are going to cover everything you need to know to make some of the tastiest beers you have ever had. And for you distillers, always remember, you get out only what you put in. If you start with a great beer you will end up with a great product!

NOTE – This book is just step one on the road to becoming a master brewer and/or distiller. It is a beginner's guide to brewing beer (and distiller's mash) and is not meant to be all things to all people. In this series I will combine art and science with some lighthearted humor to keep it fun. I will also focus strongly on one specific area in each volume, in this case Beginning Home Brewing with an emphasis on Extract Brews and Basic Fermentation concepts.

This book does not cover some of the more advanced topics such as; all grain brewing, kegging, ice jacking, specific gravity and others. I will cover those and others in the next volumes of this series.

This book is part of our FAST series of books, (Focused and Accelerate Subject Template). Ok, so I worked had to make the acronym fit, sue me.

The theory behind this format (FAST), is that few people have the inclination or desire to sit down and fully digest a 400 page instruction book in one setting. Our lives are too busy and we have too many distractions. I wanted to develop a format that allowed a person to pick up a book, read it quickly and easily comprehend the basics of whatever skill it is they want to learn. Its learning set to the pace of our mobile lifestyles. I found it is easier for me to learn this way and I hope it works for you.

Jeff King, HPC (Head Pirate in Charge)

Introduction

We all love our flags. We like our national anthems and unique national holidays, (I love you Thanksgiving!). We cherish our national traditions. And one of the biggest traditions and in fact a core to most cultures is their cuisine. What you grow up eating and drinking becomes a large part of who we are. Don't believe me? Try insulting someone's traditional beverage.

Black tea? The Brits can take it, with cream and sugar. The Chinese prefer a green tea. Italy, Spain and other warm, fertile countries should feel free to talk up their wines, red and white. The Caribbean and South America boil up rum. Central America grows the agave for their tequila. Canada... what do Canadians drink? Hot cocoa? We Americans enjoy all of those at least occasionally of course, but they're really not ours to claim.

We have our Coca-Cola and whiskeys, both objects of national pride. I love a great Bourbon myself, which is about as American as it gets. But leave it to us – the upstart, young nation of opportunity for all – to take the modest beverage of beer and elevate it to the status of art, all without taking away any of its allure of casual relaxation.
In other words, beer is for everyone. Its fun, it's casual and it goes with everything! At the same time, beer can be complex, artisanal and as varied as our melting-pot nation. Wait. I'm going to change that to our boiling-pot in honor of our love of beer.

In only the recent past, American beer earned a bad reputation as being uninteresting, bland and mostly tasteless.

It was a reputation that was earned because it's at least mostly true. Can you say Schlitz? American beers were light in flavor and color, thin-bodied and heavily carbonated. Coors and Budweiser are great examples. We even go as far as to make Coors Light and Bud Light, lightening up the already light. Don't get me wrong, on a hot summer day even I am grateful for an ice cold Bud but you have to admit that it's no wonder why we sometimes get made fun of.

But in 1979 that Jimmy Carter managed to get one thing right. He signed a law that made the home brewing of beer legal. And with that one action he put into motion the beginning of the micro-beer revolution. In as little as 10 years the tide had shifted away from such commercial products and toward more varied, quality beers. Call them microbrews or craft beers, but call them decidedly delicious. Small breweries and brew pubs have popped up in almost every neighborhood even in smaller towns, and the coolers of the beer section of most liquor stores have expanded significantly.

Most importantly for this book, many beer drinkers have also taken their love into their own hands by setting up brewing operations in their homes. Millions now consider home brewing a valid hobby and spend either a little or a whole lot of time and energy making from scratch a product that they could easily buy just down the street.

To some home brewing just doesn't make much sense. They are more than happy with what they can buy at the super markets. But for those who catch the brewing bug, it's not about the time and energy. It's about doing it yourself. About creating something you can be proud of. And best of all, it's easier than you think. In fact, anyone who can follow instructions and heat water to a boil can brew their own beer. Home brewing is about the good ole American spirit of hard work, individuality and pride of accomplishment. All those wonderful things rolled into a foamy mug of beer. Trust me, a beer you bought will never taste as good as the beer that you made yourself!

As I mentioned before, I came to alcohol production as a distiller. I have been known to make my own liquors at home, and I love trying new recipes and sipping on the fruits of my labors. Brewing beer, while in some ways very much the same, is also very different and refreshing for me. Again, it's not intimidating. Anyone can do it. Anyone can enjoy it, and there is an ever growing community of home brewers for support – and who also happen to throw great parties.

After you learn the basics, which make up the meat of this instructional manual you hold in your hands, there's no big secret to brewing. There are, though, lots of small secrets, tricks of the trade and such that will make your brewing easier and brews better. You'll find those tips throughout this book.

At the end of the day I also hope you'll have found a satisfying new hobby. Who knows, maybe, once you have mastered the art of beer making you will even fire up a still and join my friends and I over on the darker side of the brewing arts.

Cheers to that!!

A Brief History of an Old Beverage

In the beginning, there was a cave man, Lets call him Grog. He wasn't much different then you or I really. Grog's wife was always on him to make their animal-hide bed or pull a bone comb through his tangled hair. His loincloth is always wrinkled. Most importantly for his descendants, though, Grog was a bit of a slob. He was never any good at dusting, cleaning or better yet, at doing the dishes. One day he accidentally left some of his berry juice in a forgotten corner of the cave, and when he stumbled upon it again, like magic – poof! – that forgotten bit of liquid had transformed into something else, something magical. And ever since that day the Irish were doomed!

One small step for caveman. One giant leap for mankind. Needless to say, as time went by, man learned much and probably forgot much as well, but he did manage to pass down the knowledge of this magical concoction through generations of his descendants. They refined and improved this bit of accidental chemistry. They learned that this "fermentation", while complicated chemically, is even more simple than baking bread. Water + Sugar + Yeast, the only hard part is the waiting.

Grapes and other fruit are a two-in-one. They have the water plus they have sugar built in. Grains are usually soaked in water and then converted into sugar through boiling.

Lastly, in Grog's day and for centuries, the yeast part of the process was wild, meaning floating around in the air. That's right, wild yeast just lives on the wind, and that made it unpredictable at best. You set out your pot and whatever yeast made its way in is what you got. As such it was always a different type and that made for different results. What was predictable is that anywhere there is sugar, wild yeast will wiggle in somehow to fulfill the sacred task of making alcohol. Later, Grog's descendants figured out that adding some of the lees from the last batch of beer sped up the fermentation process, though they still had no idea how or why the process worked.

Sumerian receipt for "best" beer from a brewer, c. 2050 BC

Actually, some smart people more educated than I (Ok, so that's not saying much) think that one of the most important outcomes of humans settling down from being hunter-gatherers and becoming stationary agriculturalists was beer. We traded bows and arrows for hoes and plows, and why? At least in part: beer.

In areas of the Mediterranean like Italy and Greece, grapes grow easy and plentiful, so they stuck with their wines. In climates where grains grew best, they made beer – and with whatever grains were at hand. In Asia, they fermented rice. In Africa, they used millet. In Northern Europe, they used mostly barley, and that is the heritage that has been passed on through the centuries to modern day America.

Nowadays, we think of beer as something fun. We drink it to relax or celebrate. We drink beer that suits our food or the season. Yes, we drink it for the buzz, but those reasons are not the ones that made beer so important for people in the past. They drank the stuff because it was safer than drinking the water. There was no purification of the water back in the day. More often than not, that same river or pond where people washed their clothes, bathed and threw out their sewage was also the same place where they got their drinking water. Drinking the water could literally kill you. Enter BEER!

Beer has to be boiled in the process of mashing and guess what boiling does... Yep, it kills almost all of those nasty germs. It did not take Grog and his family long to learn that drinking the water made you sick but if you drank beer you were fine. Hell, you were better than fine.

PRO TIP: When traveling with your spouse feel free to use that as an excuse. "But honey I have to stay hydrated and you know what they say about the water here".

Beer was also nutrition. It was and still is sometimes called "liquid bread". Rations of beer nourished the people that sweated in the hot sun to build the pyramids. Boats loaded on tons of beer for their sailors, who needed the hydration and the 600 or so calories you could pack in a day if you drank a pint at every meal.

For a long time, all brewing was home brewing. Beer kind of went hand in hand with making bread, another of life's staples, if not as intoxicating. The same wheat pounded and processed by hand to make flour for the bread in the oven was thrown into water on top of the fire. Even better, the malted grain leftover from making beer could be used as a base for more bread. And when the bread started to go bad it could go in the pot to make beer. Ah, the circle of life!

Because they could not bottle it families had to make beer on a regular basis or it would spoil. As people settled down to form villages it became apparent that some people were better at some chores than others. This formed the basis for the separation of labor that spawned the birth of trades. Maybe not the "oldest" profession but certainly in the top 10 was that of brewer. Everyone can make a beer but not everyone is good at it. Whether it was a secret recipe, special yeast that they had found or just that they just had a knack for it, some people were just better at brewing than others. So naturally those families would end up selling their tastier beers to those less talented.

Women were incredibly important in the process. The lady of the house was usually in charge of cooking and baking. Brewing was all in the same category as far as families were concerned. Women's work! Those who were good at it were called alewives and ran what was basically the first open taps out of their kitchens. Bring your jug and get in line at the kitchen door folks.

These people didn't have downright horrible taste in their beer. They cared about flavor and aroma. They experimented by throwing different things into the mix, like ginger, anise (think black licorice) and juniper. Hops came along later, but it landed with a big bang and revolutionized beer history. Sure, hops adds its signature bitter flavor that we know so well in beers today, but hops also acted as a stabilizer in beer! It didn't go bad nearly as quickly!

We have religion to thank for that big breakthrough. Specifically, it was the monks, at least for the most part. In a time when life was short and filled with not much else than hard work, they were the kind of people who had time on their hand to try new things and even keep accurate records of their brewing experiments, all in an effort to make a better beer. They had the patience to work on isolating better yeast rather than relying on wild strains and to use that yeast, which liked colder places, to create beers that needed to age for a significant amount of time in the cool, dry basements of their monasteries. Those were the first lagers. German for "to store" is "lagern."

So then we had two types of beer. The kind fermented the old way (which eventually would be called 'top fermented,' then without hops) and this new, aged beer (eventually called 'bottom fermented,' with hops). The old stuff had always been called ale. The new stuff actually got the name "beer" that came to be associated with all types of grain-based fermented brews. We think ales are a type of beer. Drinkers in those days would have violently disagreed.

If we jump over to American history, beer has been with us from the very beginning. It was standard practice for all ships (even the Nina, Pinta and Santa Maria as well as the Mayflower) to carry onboard three times the amount of beer as they did water. The first Puritan settlers were so in need of beer that they tried brewing it with things like pumpkins and even parsnips before they got grain to grow easily in the New World. Desperate people and all that. Remember that old story about the Indians teaching the Puritans to grow corn? Yeah, they tried that too. Didn't make much of a beer but we found other things to use it for latter!

By the time of the American Revolution, home brewing and small-scale commercial brewing was widespread. George Washington besides being the largest distiller of the time also famously wrote down a recipe for his house beer. Thomas Jefferson brewed (or rather, had one of his servants brew) beer at Monticello. Samuel Adams, as the modern beer named after him suggests, was a brewer by trade.

What's more, the Founding Fathers didn't just brew and imbibe beer. The revolution itself was centered on beer. Revolutionaries met at local taverns, which were the hub of social and political life of every town and neighborhood. Taverns were where you went to get news, where strangers new in town would go first, and where you could cook up plans and schemes in whispers over your suds. It's likely that the patriots who dumped tea in the Boston Harbor at the famous Tea Party met for a liquid courage beforehand and for some celebratory brews afterward at their local tavern. Face it, beer is more American than apple pie.

These were pretty much all ales, mind you, though they did include hops by that point in addition to malted barley. It wasn't until the 1840s that lagers became the big thing in America. That's the time period when loads of German immigrants jumped the pond to start their lives over in the New World, and they brought with them their taste for the aged, hopped-up beer. They settled in cities like, St. Louis, Milwaukee, Cincinnati and they brought their lagers with them.

Then in the 1870s, the scientists Pasteur and Hansen studied fermentation and made some interesting discoveries about yeast. For one, they finally figured out that this little, living organism of yeast was the drive behind fermentation. Plus, other organisms that got into the mix through contamination could throw the yeast off its game. Quickly, yeast was captured and commoditized. Even your corner general store could sell you powdered or liquid yeast, pure and packaged and ready to go. Brewers didn't need to rely upon the wild yeasts that float around in the air naturally or yeast isolated from previous batches. That purity and precision meant brewers had more standardized, better quality batches. Before, some reported that they usually threw out one in five batches because it was bad and undrinkable, and they previously had no idea why.

But all this technical innovation and the age and space required for lagering made brewing harder and harder to do at home. Plus, there were all sorts of taverns selling the stuff right down the street – and it was better stuff than the unskilled Joe could brew in his kitchen – and home brewing began its long, sad decline into obscurity.

If beer was once thought of as a good alcohol keeping people away from the evil stuff, that all changed and changed hard in the 20th Century. There was this big, grand and inevitably disastrous experiment called the Temperance Movement, which led to Prohibition in 1920. No alcohol, not even beer, could be made, transported or consumed in America. They were well meaning folk but you know what they say about good intentions. Sadly it's one tradgedy our government has failed to learn. Even today, though it's legal to make wine and beer, home distilling is still banned. Why? Well they will say it's to keep you safe. The truth is more likely found in their bank account. But I digress.

This was devastating and tragic for American brewing, of course. It was a long, dark period of forced "sobriety" that lasted 14 long, dark years. But it was particularly bad for beer. In 1876, there were 2,600 breweries in America. In 1933 at the end of Prohibition, there were only 700 left. Only the big, bad boys with deep pockets survived, driving out local breweries and mom-and-pop operations. Then the big boys ate one another and got even bigger over the decades, until in 1976, there were less than 40 breweries in all of the United States. How un-American is that?

It was during that time that American beers took what most beer lovers think of as a huge nosedive into light, bubbly blandness. Part of that trend is built in to our climate. There are parts of the U.S. that get hella hot and stay that way most of the year. Most people like to drink light, refreshing beers in the heat. Dark beers were out and light, unobtrusive pilsners were in.

On top of that, we Americans were gung ho on making food production all fancy and modern so we could make more, make it faster and make it safer. Canned food, frozen food, packaged food. So just like how we got bland white bread, we began to get bland light beer, because producers were catering to the lowest common denominator in tastes.

World War II didn't help much either. With all the men abroad, beer makers went even lighter to try to make beer drinkers out of the women who stayed home. Rosie the Riveter deserved a drink and they were going to sell her what she wanted. Or at least what they thought she wanted.

After Prohibition, the law had specifically made it clear that people could once again make wine in their own homes. No one said anything about beer, though, and so home brewing was still illegal. But a small few kept at it, in the dark of their basement they kept the craft alive. Then in 1979, President Carter signed a law giving beer back to the people. Once again you could brew at home and you could brew up to 200 gallons a year in a household of two people.

PRO TIP: That's a little more than two pints a day per person. Totally manageable!

And in drips and drabs – more recently in a rushing torrent – Americans have come full circle, once again home brewing is where it's at. Microbreweries and brew pubs have popped up like weeds. Even the average Joe has tried ales, lagers, stouts, porters and pilsners, and beer geeks can go off on lambics, saisons and barley wines. You can buy home brew kits at Wal-Mart these days. Note I said "can" and not "should". These are less brewing kits and more closely related to, say, instant coffee.

This resurgence goes hand in hand with Americans' demand for quality and artisanship in all their foodstuffs, from their organic vegetables to their farm-raised chickens, artisan sausages and hand-churned butters. And thankfully, these new beers suit those sorts of tastes just fine. There is a brew for every season and for every style of cooking, elevating the enjoyment of beer to the level that wine has enjoyed for so long.

That brings us to today. The home brewer is no longer some crackpot hiding in his basement. Welcome to the new America, where it's estimated that up to 1 million people brew beer in their homes at least once a year and there are 30,000 members of the American Home Brewers Association. Home brewing has gone from being a staple of every day life to underground resistance and back into the light of day. Today home brewers are well known for their artisanal brews and top shelf tastes.

Ok, enough with the history lessons lets get down to business and talk about how we make beer today!

The Drunken Chemist

Beer and laziness go hand in hand, at least in stereotypes. We think of people like the pot-bellied dude kicked back in a La-Z-Boy watching football, or grilling up burgers and shooting the breeze at a backyard barbecue, both with beers in their hands. For a long time beer was considered the drink of the common man while wine was for the intelligent high-class connoisseur. Beer was considered the drink of the baseball-loving, peanut-eating masses.

I'm proud to say that despite those preconceived ideas, brewers are actually chemists. They're overseeing a fascinating and complex chemical reaction. And as for being dumb, well, it's actually a more complex process to make beer than to make wine, so put that in your stem glass.

Both alcoholic beverages – and really, you drink whatever floats your boat, more power to you – are the products of fermentation. Fermentation is the process of changing sugar into alcohol. In the case of wine, grapes are a fruit and therefore already contain sugar naturally. They're primed and loaded to be made alcoholic. Beer, on the other hand, is built from starches and little proteins in grains like barley, wheat, oats and rye.

So there's this whole extra step that must take place before fermentation can begin, and that's turning our grain from a starch into a sugar and we do this with malt. We'll talk a little more about malting later, but the simple version is that you take your grain, usually barley, and you soak it in water until it starts to germinate, or sprout. Now, the grain thinks it's about to be supporting new life in the form of a brand new plant, so it starts to make special enzymes that break down starches and proteins into simple sugars, which are easier for the new plant to consume in order to grow. In straight talk, the enzymes make sugary baby plant food.

But rather than letting the plant grow, the germination is stopped there and the grain is dried out, keeping our precious enzymes intact and bringing them up to the natural state of grapes, meaning containing the building blocks of alcohol.

Then we start the fermentation, which depends solely on one important organism: yeast. I think about the yeast as one of those competitive eaters you see on TV stuffing their faces full or hot dogs or pie. They're insanely hungry, and their food is sugar. They eat and eat, literally until they die. In fact, those fat, dead little yeast monsters have to be strained out later. Before they kick the bucket, though, they leave the waste products of all their binge sugar eating in the form of ethyl alcohol and carbon dioxide gas (for bubbly carbonation).

PRO TIP: When a yeast eats sugars it grows and multiplies, that is as long as it has access to oxygen. But if you deprive that yeast of oxygen it becomes anaerobic and gives off alcohol instead!

This fermentation process starts off strong when you begin a new batch of home brew, then it slows down but continues over the course of days and weeks as the beer sits in cold storage.

It sounds foolproof, but yeast is picky. The fermentation of the sugar won't kick off if the conditions are too hot or too cold, or if there's too little or too much sugar to consume. There are methods and tools that can help you make the right conditions for perfect fermentation, things like thermometers and hydrometers (used to measure the density of water) and precise scales to weigh ingredients. Those are all great. We need those.

But don't forget that as much as this is a chemical process, brewing beer can also be an art form. Every brewer has the opportunity to tweak something here, substitute something there, and experiment to his or her heart's content. Even when you follow a recipe, you leave your unique fingerprint on every batch. No one can likely recreate exactly your beer in exactly the same way, so don't let a little bit of chemistry dampen your enthusiasm for this most excellent and creative hobby. Remember, if Grog could do this, than so can you.

You should note that there are essentially 3 ways to make beer:

The instant beer kit. These are those kits you see in big box stores with a brown plastic "keg". It's like making cake from a box mix. You open packet one, mix in water, add packet two and put it in the fridge. I will not be covering this method.

Extract Brewing (EB). This is the topic that we will cover the most in this book. Essentially the grains are used only for flavoring and the malt extract is added for it's sugar and the conversion of the remaining sugars. This can be done easily in one pot and is by far the best way to get good beers in reasonable amount of time.

All Grain (AG). In AG you use either pre-malted grains or you can malt them yourself. With this method you have the most control, you can get an optimum conversion rate, you can produce a much tastier product and it takes much longer. Also it requires very, VERY specific temperature controls. On top of that it requires more equipment as it is usually done in a three pot system.

Ok well more like 3.1 is BIAB (Brew In A Bag). This is a type of AG brewing that really took off in Australia. It turns the typical 3 pot system used in AG into a one pot system like in EB. You put all your grains into a bag (Such as cheesecloth) and cook it like you would in AG but then instead of a full lautering process you just pull the grains out and then sparg with hot water. While this is an excellent alternative and I'm a big fan of it, really it deserves it's own book. For all the problems that it solves it brings a whole new load of challenges to the home brewer.

If you do decide to go the BIAB route I highly recommend the bags over at http://www.bagbrewer.com He sent me a couple bags to test out and I have to say they are the best made I've seen.

Great Grains

When I hear the word grain, I think about wavy fields of the stuff growing in a sunny field in Iowa. I see it in its natural state, and that's what you're going to see beer companies advertise of their labels and billboards, too. Pretty pictures of grains in the sun. By the time they get to you though these grains will have most like gone through an intense processing phase.

As I said, the process is called malting and it is overseen by someone called the Maltster. I kid you not, that is what they're really called. These people, too, are artisans. They know their stuff and their part of the malting process makes a big difference in what you'll be swigging from your frosty mug.

We start with the soaking of the grain until germination – and how long the grain germinates affects your beer – followed by a drying out period. This usually happens in a kiln, which is really just a big oven. It used to be that the kiln was heated by open fire, and the flavor of the grains was changed based on what you used as fuel for the fire, such as the type of wood. Did you know that Scotch whiskey gets its unique flavor because to this day it's malted over peat fires? That's why it tastes just like the Home & Garden center at Home Depot. Ok, so I'm not a fan of Scotch, moving on. Today we use heated air, which some people say does remove a smokey element that used to be common in beer. Good or a bad, let nothing stand in the way of progress, right?

That drying period is important. The higher the temperature and the longer the grain spends in the kiln, the darker and more caramelized the flavor of the resulting beer. So the less time and lower the temperature, the lighter and crisper the beer will be. Plus, the longer it dries, allowing the sugars to caramelize, also makes the color of the beer darker. No matter what, the product that comes out at the end is our malt, and malt is the keystone of beer.

The vast majority of the time, you'll be working with malted barley. In fact, 30 percent of all the barley produced in the world gets malted in some way, whether for beer, liquor or another product. There's good reason for that. Barley beers are stable, relatively easy to make and just taste damn good.

There are two main types, two-row and six-row barley. They're named for the number of kernels on the head of the grain. The difference is that two-row barley will make a beer that's cleaner and perhaps softer, whereas a six-row beer can be more tannic but takes well to flavor additives sometimes added later in the fermentation. There's also barley planted in the spring versus barley planted in the winter, and there are slightly different types of barley that grow in different climates.

All those little things are tools to personalize and experiment with beer, and create an infinite number of possible combinations. The final product, the malted grain, will eventually be combined with water during the first stage of your brewing process to create what's called the wort.

Right now, you're probably picturing a pile of grain, maybe not whole heads of grain but recognizable chopped up or mashed pieces of grain. That does exist. We call it "grain malt," and it looks somewhat like what it's made from. But leave it to modern man to take that old-fashioned process and make it even easier. You can say, "Thank you" to modern man later, because he seriously improved your future brewing life, trust me. Rather than using only or mostly grain malts, malt extracts are now readily available both in your local home-brew store and all over the Internet.

PRO TIP: The bulk of the cost of malts as well as hops and other brewing ingredients is shipping. It's worth checking out your local store, the prices might be more competitive than you would think. Plus, your home-brew store comes stocked with real-life, human brewers who are more than happy to share their love of the craft with other masters and even beginner's like yourself.

PRO TIP PART DEUX: 99% of the people who work in home brew stores are "Beer Geeks". They seek to find others and make them like themselves, kind of like vampires. Understand that when you start a conversation with one of them you many need to chew off your own ankle to get away.

Malt extract begins its life in the same way that grain malts do. They're soaked in water until they reach the desired stage of germination. Then they veer off their own way because they're ground into grist and placed in sealed vacuum evaporators. These machines suck all but 20 percent of the water out of the wort, leaving behind a whoppingly strong 80 percent sugar solids. Talk about locked and loaded for alcohol production! Grain malts are still readily available, and are used by many home brewers. However, malt extracts are a wonderful beer-making tool, and that's doubly true for your first efforts at making beer. Extracts subtract many steps from the complicated process of all grain brewing.

Extracts usually come in three ways: liquid in a can, as syrup or in powdered form. Some are even hopped extracts, meaning the hops element is pre-built-in for you – and you can skip the upcoming section on hops in those cases – so read labels carefully.

PRO TIP: Especially with your first few batches, I'd stick with the malt extract syrup. Granted, the powdered extract is easier to measure out and easier to clean up, but powdered extract needs to be stored air-tight and moisture-free in a big way, which is easy to mess up and ruin a whole bag of the stuff.

DISTILLER'S TIP: If you are making a "distiller's beer" then don't use the pre "hopped" verity. Typically distillers do not use hops. The bitter flavor that they provide to the beer becomes overwhelming when distilled.

Extracts are simple, easy to store and to transport. Today thanks to the home-brew Renaissance, you can easily find malt extracts like Brewfern from Belgium, Brewmaker from England, Cooper from Australia, Laaglande from Holland and Mountmellic from Ireland.

There are people who want to and successfully do malt at home from scratch. More power to them! But don't feel as if you're missing out on the artisan process because half of the work is done for you before fermentation even begins. Malting is hard. It takes a lot of time and a lot of space, and usually costs MORE than buying the product premade. Even many large commercial breweries buy their grains from the large malting companies. Only the big boys can afford their own in-house malting operations. It just makes sense to make use of this convenient ingredient that's right at your fingertips.

Like I said, the vast majority of malts are going to be barley, which makes a beer many describe as clean and slightly sweet. That doesn't mean barley is your only option, though.

WHEAT

Wheat beers are more tart and citric in flavor. The grain is harder to germinate and malt because it doesn't have a husk and is therefore more delicate.

Wheat beers were once available almost exclusively in Belgium and Germany until about the 1980s, but since then many Americans (or at least Americans into craft and microbrews) have fallen in love with wheat. All-wheat beers are still relatively rare in the home brewing world. They're notorious unstable in clarity, meaning the beer can be very cloudy. More often, wheat is added to a base of malted barley to create a grain hybrid that tastes of the wheat without the extra work of making an all-wheat beer.

OATS

Easy to grow and plentiful, oats are a tempting fermenting grain. Oats are also tricky, though. They have a lot of protein, oil and fat, more than barley. It's more difficult to draw their sugars out in the malting process and they absorb a lot of water when cooking.

RYE

Rye is pretty uncommon in beer for many of the same reasons as wheat. It's hard to malt because of its fragility and also because rye has lots of sticky and gummy components. These gum up and clog malting equipment, which makes the Maltsters super unhappy. When made, rye beers can be strong and slightly spicy.

Grains are not only used as the base of beers, though. There's usually a barley base, of course. There are also additives – things that you put in on top of the barley malt to add flavor, aroma or other qualities – that brewers call "adjuncts." An adjunct is defined as "any cereal grain or fermentable ingredient added to the mash." These can add flavor or otherwise change the nature of the beer, making it clearer or faster to ferment, to give two examples.

For instance, you can take a barley malt base and add wheat as an adjunct to get lots of wheat flavor without the wheat headache. The wheat adds a crisp, sometimes citrusy or banana-like flavor. Oat flakes added into a dark, caramelized barley mash create wonderful oatmeal stouts.

By far the most common adjuncts, though, are corn and rice. Those are not the first two grains to spring to mind when talking about beer, I know. So why are they so common? For one, corn and rice are CHEAP, so profits are high for the beer companies who use them. Who cares about taste when they can make $0.005 cents more per can?

But even I admit there are reasons to add corn and/or rice. It makes for a lighter, snappier beer, and also helps the stability of the beer. In other words, you wind up with a beer that's clearer, stores better for longer and is less filling but without having lowered the alcohol content. Americans like their light, less filling beers, so someone is going to make a brew that meets that demand, after all. Actually, American beers are known to be between 30-40 percent adjuncts in general.

Other adjuncts have different purposes. Some clarify. Some create a foamier head. Others are there simply for the enjoyment of their aroma or flavor. Brewers have long added ingredients like fruits, herbs, spices, honey or syrups, and those are considered adjuncts, too.

The one adjunct that's easily the most controversial is sugar. This could be in grain or syrup form. Obviously, more sugar means more food for the yeast and therefore sometimes a higher alcohol content. Dark sugars can add some flavor characteristics, but sugar in general is used to reduce the chance of hazy beer and reduce the body of the beer. The result is a thinner, dryer brew.

Lots of brewers think sugar should come nowhere near your wort. In terms of lagers, I think that's 100 percent true. Ales are a different story, though. Brewers have been adding sugar to ale recipes for more than a century, so what's good enough for the masters is good enough for me – if it's the right amount in the right recipe.

Grains! They are what makes beer great and are the very foundation of any beer. They're also numerous and varied, with lots of possible combinations and flavors. Don't be intimidated by them. The KISS (keep it simple, stupid) method can totally work here, because simple beers can be nonetheless spectacular. Start with the basics. Later you can always work your way though the specialty malts and adjuncts. There's nowhere to go but up.

Water, Water Everywhere

What is the number one ingredient in Beer? Yep, it's water. Now that may seem obvious yet some people are still surprised to learn that more than 90 percent of the volume of beer is made up of water. That means that 90 percent of the quality of your beer depends upon the taste and quality of your water.

The big brewers not only know this but also take advantage of the fact. Coors and Anheuser-Busch both have TV commercials that show the clear, rushing water of their (alleged) sources and brag about how much it affects taste and quality. Brewing at home does not lessen the importance of the ingredient. Think about water as the blank canvas on which you as an artist are going to throw your paints (grains, hops, yeast) to create your masterpiece.

Most Americans turn on their water taps to municipal water, meaning its water pumped and regulated by the local government. A lot of municipal water is severely over-chlorinated to the point where you can taste it, because chlorine kills bacteria and makes the water safer overall without damaging people's health (too much). If that's the case with your water, boiling it before use can steam off some of that nasty tang.

Municipal water, like all water really, also contains minerals. Some minerals are great. Too many of certain minerals can be harmful, though. They affect not only taste but can also mess with the chemical reactions necessary for fermentation. Running your water through a carbon filter – like those found in Britta pitchers and the like – removes most common contaminants and makes water taste better.

PRO TIP: Both boiling and filtering add time to your brewing process, especially because the water should be cool or cold when you start. When they're brewing regularly, many home brewers keep a few gallons of ready water in the fridge to make brewing faster and easier. If you have to treat your water, try to do it the day or night before you plan on making your beer to make it easier on yourself.

The great thing about having municipal water, though, is that there's someone to call to get your water tested. In most cases, you can get your water tested at least once every so often for absolutely free.

If you have well water at your house, well, there's a little more involved. The risk of biological contaminants – those nasties the chlorine in municipal water kills – is much, much higher. You should definitely have your water tested, which will cost a bit because you'll have to hire a tester out of your own pocket. Even so, you should only have to test once every couple of years, unless something drastic changes in the meantime.

If your water is no good, you can always outsource the problem and beg/borrow/steal/buy your water elsewhere, whether from friends or retail. By "no good" I mean water that you don't even like to drink on a daily basis. Spring water is ideal. Water from friends out in the country or in different water systems might be of better quality. DO NOT use distilled water, though. It lacks any little bit of minerals, and some quantity of those is necessary for the brewing process.

Again, if you like to drink it, it's probably good for beer making. If you want to go the extra mile to make sure, many home brewers opt to pH test their water. A thing's pH is a measurement of its acidity on a scale of 1-13. A 7 is considered neutral. Anything lower is more acidic, and anything higher is less acidic.

Alcohols in general are just a touch on the acid side. Wine rates a 3 or 4 pH. Beer rates about 4-4.5 pH, though it's about 5-5.5 pH prior to fermentation. You can buy pH-testing strips from your local homebrew store, and most likely, your water is totally in the acceptable range that won't interfere with the fermenting process. If it's too high or too low, there are solutions. Adding small amounts of calcium can lower pH, and calcium carbonate can raise the pH number, for instance.

The cheapest and simplest way to good water if it doesn't happen to flow from your tap, though, is to beg, borrow or steal it. Ok, so don't "steal" it. Just offer to compensate the family or friends you borrow it from with some of the homebrew results, and most people are more than happy to lend you a hand or a bucket as it were.

Hops To It

As I talked about when we went through the history of beer, hops were a late player in the brewing game. It's been used on and off since the 13th Century, but only regularly for the last 150-200 years. Before that, hops' main use was as stuffing for pillows because it was thought to make you drowsy and help you sleep better. Oh well. Beer can make you drowsy in its own way, and it's definitely more satisfying than a fragrant pillow.

Hops are not strictly necessary for brewing. Well, it's not necessary for fermentation to take place and alcohol to form. It is necessary to our modern beer palates, because it would not taste like beer to us without the aromatic, bitter herb. Beer without hops would feel flabby on the tongue and one-note. It would feel too simple and, in many cases, too sweet.

DISTILLER'S TIP: Skip this chapter! Ok, you still might want to read it but remember hops are bitter and distilling concentrates flavor. Do you really want bitter whiskey? Well maybe, but that's up to you. In general you can take any good beer recipe and remove the hops and make a great whiskey out of it.

For a long, long time before hops were used regularly home brewers added a bunch of different plants to their beers. Why did hops become not only the herb of choice but also a necessity? Four reasons:

- Hops stabilize beer so it doesn't go bad as fast, especially if stored in the right conditions.
- Hops clarify brews, making them less cloudy than the old styles of ales
- Hops create and keep a nice head on the beer.
- Hops are unique in that it bonds with unwanted malt proteins and pulls those out of suspension so the brewer can remove them easily.

Does the average home brewer need to know all those things in order to make good beer? Hops will work its chemistry even if you don't know how the science works. But knowing a bit about the important ingredient will help you understand how tweaking the type of hops and your hopping method can drastically change the character of your beer – and offer lots of room for creativity.

Hops are a member of the nettle family. Hops are also cousins with cannabis, aka marijuana. Oh, Mother Nature does have a sense of humor, one family of plants being the basis for so much fun.

There are lots of different kinds of hops, mainly because hops have been adapted to grow in so many different climates, from the United Kingdom through Germany, Belgium, Australia, New Zealand, Japan and the Pacific Northwest of the United States. The U.K. is the No. 1 producer of the herb, followed by the U.S. at No. 2. In the US, Washington state leads in terms of American hops production.

Hops are grown like most other crops, out in the fields with the natural sun and rain. So just like grapes, there can be good years and bad years for hops. That doesn't mean you need to start slapping a "vintage" date or anything on your beer like wine does, but it's still vital to know in order to brew at your best.

It's also vital to understand the effects of different kinds of hops. There are no right and wrong types, of course, because that depends on the kind of beer you're making as well as your personal tastes. But people needed a way to talk about and measure the differences between different types, so they created International Bitterness Units. The IBU rating shows the level of something called the herb's alpha acids. Alpha acids are almost entirely responsible for a beer's bitterness, so the higher the IBU, the more bitter the hops.

More recently, there came about an even better measurement for our needs, that of the Homebrew Bitterness Unit, or HBUs. This is likely the measurement you'll see on packaging and use in planning your beer batches. The HBU is the percentage of alpha acids multiplied by the amount of hops in ounces. (Alpha * ounces = HBU.) Big, commercial brewers use IBUs to find one or two consistent types of hops that they use to make sure all their beers are of uniform quality and taste. You get to use HBUs to do the exact opposite: to create the spiciness of life in the form of variety.

Seriously, the variety is endless. Yes, there are all sorts of different kinds of hops based on climate, year and bitterness. Factor in the different ways you can add hops to your brew, and number of possibilities grows exponentially.

You see, hops can be added to your wort at any time in the beer-making process. There are two main categories of timing, though.

BITTERING OR BOILING HOPS
These hops are added your wort at the very beginning or near to the beginning. It's called boiling hops because it will definitely be boiled with the wort, though for varying amounts of time. These hops are allowed to really steep and add their deep character to the beer and most affect its final flavor. Most

of the time, this method will boil the hops anywhere from 20 minutes to up to an hour (for lagers) or two hours (for ales), though recipes vary.

AROMATIC OR FINISHING HOPS
These hops are added at or near the end of the fermenting process. It doesn't have time to add deep character to the taste, but it's excellent for adding a wonderful aroma and even spice to your beer. Finishing hops can be added at the end of the boil when the wort is still hot or it can go as far as dry hopping. Dry hopping means adding the hops to the aging container.

It's often the case that the home brewer will add more than one kind of hops and more than once during the brewing process. Dogfish Head Ales even came up with a continuess method of adding hops. Their 60 and 90 IPAs refer to the length of time that hops are added.

PRO TIP: Every home brewer should have a journal or spreadsheet where he or she writes down everything they used and did for every different batch. This includes a list of the ingredients, all of which are important, but hops is the most important. There are so many different types and different methods/timing to introduce the hops. It's easy to lose track completely if you don't keep careful records.

PRO, PRO TIP: Write all that stuff down as you go along and BEFORE you start drinking it!

Just like with malts, American home brewers can find hops in different forms. The ones we use most often are loose or leaf hops, hops pellets and hops extract. Hops also come with a scale of its storage or keeping quality. If it goes bad or becomes stale quickly, it ranks poor. Average keeping is ranked fair. Those that keep well are ranked good.

LOOSE/LEAF HOPS

Loose hops are as close as you can get to taking the plant directly out of the fields. Growers bundle up their hops crop in big, compressed bales. Many larger home-brew stores and retailers will buy by the quarter bale and then repackage that into smaller units better suited to the needs of small-scale brewers like you.

What the hops looks and feels like will show you its freshness. The plant has a yellow powder called lupulin that's the source of a lot of hops' power of bitterness and sterilization. Do you see that powder? How the bales were compressed might affect the quality of the powder. The hops should be greenish yellow and not crackly to the touch. Even the most expensive, best type of hops is worth little if it's old and stale.

PRO TIP: Ask your home-brew store or contact your online retailer to ask about how their hops are stored, both by them and before it came into their hands. At the very minimum, it should be dated and hopefully refrigerated. Ask before you buy or you may be disappointed in the quality you receive. Even cheaper hops, though, can make decent beers. It's all a matter of what you're aiming for.

HOPS PELLETS

These pellets, which look a little like rabbit food, are made by grinding the hops into grist and compressing them. This makes them much easier to store. For the best results and longest freshness, all hops should be refrigerated or (the best way) frozen. Pelletized hops are more stable. You still need to store them with care, but there's less chance of losing an entire batch due to one small mistake or problem.

Pelletized hops also has the benefit of needing less boil time and having a larger percentage of alpha yield, which means it gives up more of its alpha acids for bitterness.

PRO TIP: Even with hops pellets, it pays to take precautions when storing your hops. The delicate little herb can absorb the odors and flavors of whatever is around it, which means it could soak up the funk of your Chinese take-out or casserole leftovers, especially in the fridge but even in the freezer. Take the extra time to double wrap your hops so it keeps the character and qualities you paid for.

HOPS EXTRACT
This type of hops is the most processed. In order to make the liquid, it's often dissolved in hexane or boiled in alkaline water. I don't like using products with big, scientific-y words that I don't understand – and neither do some other home brewers. Extracts are generally used when a bigger brewer wants consistency and simplicity, but especially when you're just starting out, there is nothing wrong with experimenting with the extracts. Whatever will get you on the home-brewing bandwagon is cool with me.

A last word on hops: With the rise in popularity of home brewing, suppliers of home-brewing ingredients have tried to make the process really easy to learn for beginners. One result is pre-hopped malt extracts, which I mentioned before. The hops are built in. At least, the boiling hops are built in. They add the needed bitterness, but with little aroma or finer characteristics. You can still put finishing hops on top of that base, but hopped extracts are a one-stop-shop way to go to make decent, drinkable but not upscale or complex beers. Ah, the ease of modern man. Maybe such simple, packaged easiness is not what you aspire to, but it's not all bad. Everyone has to start somewhere.

Hungry, Happy Yeast

Yeast, the competitive eating single-celled organism that makes fermentation and therefore beer possible. I've used the word magic to describe what the little buggers do, and magic is the right word for it. For centuries, people knew they needed malted grain and water, but then thought that… well, that fermentation just happened, it was an act of the gods. Sure, there was this gray scummy stuff to scrape off your batch of beer (which was dead yeast, of course), but that was just something that happened.

Even after the microscope was invented, it took a while for Pasteur and friends to isolate yeast, and then it took much convincing to make people believe that it was yeast that made the magic happen. Thankfully, very quickly after that, isolated and sterile yeast was available all over the place, including in your neighborhood general store. This was what we now think of as baker's yeast, which you use to make bread and which does trigger beer fermentation. The waste products of yeast eating sugar in fermentation, remember, are alcohol and carbon dioxide. When you're baking a loaf of bread, the alcohol cooks off and the carbon dioxide gas is the force that causes the bread to rise. And yes you "can" use baker's yeast to make beer. But remember much of the taste of your beer comes from the yeast. I've tasted some bakers yeast brews and trust me, there is a reason brewers don't use those today.

Five hundred unique strains of yeast have now been discovered and isolated. We know a great deal more about how the little bugger lives and how it dies. For example, yeast can reproduces up to 30 times – can make 30 more little yeasties – before it dies. In theory, then, one single yeast cell could be put in a batch of beer and kick off a chain of reproduction that would eventually ferment the whole batch. In practice, though, adding enough yeast is key. It needs numbers to fight the other inevitable microbes as well as insure its own reproduction and the chances of fermentation success.

PRO TIP: When yeasts have food, water and oxygen they reproduce like crazy. When you deprive them of that oxygen, like say when you put an airlock on something, they become anaerobic and instead of reproducing they make alcohol. So if you want to grow your yeast, give them plenty of air. Cap off that air when it's time to brew.

Today, we've refined the use of yeast specifically for the beer-brewing process to make the final product and the process the best possible. There are two kinds of yeast used for home brewing.

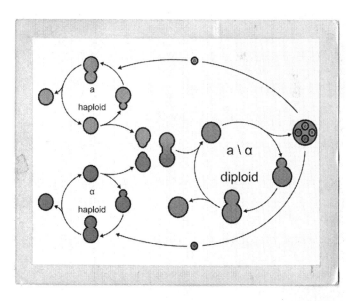

(Yeast Life Cycle)

SACCHAROMYCES CEREVISIAE

Cerevisiae is the modern version of top-fermenting yeast used to make ales, the older form of brewing before lagers came along. It ferments in warmer temperatures – 55-75 degrees Fahrenheit – than its sister uvarum. It also has a higher alcohol tolerance (higher ABV!) and creates a slightly sweeter beer. It's excellent when aiming for English-style ales, porters and stouts.

Anymore, it's not strictly top fermenting, though. It does start out fermenting at the top of whatever vessel you're using to make beer, but then it will fall to the bottom when fermentation is complete and the yeast is dead.

SACCHAROMYCES UVARUM

Uvarum is the modern perfection of the old bottom-fermenting method that created the lager class of beers. It ferments in cooler temperature of 32-55 degrees Fahrenheit, and true to the name, it settles relatively quickly to the bottom of your fermenting vessel. The result is brighter and more complex beer with deeper flavors. It's great when you're trying to brew up lagers, of course. Uvarum, however, can be a bit more fragile than cerevisiae.

PRO TIP: Most home brewers, especially those who are rookies, stick to ale yeast and are more than happy with the quality of their beers and the variety of beers they can make. A temperature of lower than 55 degrees but higher than freezing at 32 degrees is hard to maintain around the house. Maybe you have a basement or a garage that can do the trick, but again, can you guarantee it will never freeze? In fact, lots of experts say lagers didn't really take off until refrigeration was invented because they were difficult to keep at the right temperature without the modern convenience of the fridge. Don't feel obligated or shame about not using lager yeasts, especially in the first few years of your home-brewing experience.

The fancy measurement we use to talk about yeasts (because we always need a fancy word to use, right?) is its attenuation range, meaning its ability to metabolize malt sugars. In language I better understand, the attenuation range number is the percentage of the all the sugar in the wort that yeast will eat before it shuts down and dies. Most home-brewers' yeasts have a range of about 65-85 percent.

As with most other home-brewing ingredients, you can buy your yeast in a couple of different forms.

DRY YEAST
This is powdered yeast. It usually comes in sealed, sterile envelopes, in which the yeast is dormant. In order to wake the buggers up, you have to add it to warm water. Dry yeast is the way to go for novice home brewers. It's the cheapest option, for one, but it also requires less specialized knowledge. One package of dry yeast can also bring an average-sized batch up to 9 percent ABV.

LIQUID YEAST
This yeast is already active when you buy it, in test tubes or foil packs. It's available in great regional varieties like British, Belgian, Irish and German, but it's also more expensive and trickier to use. One portion of liquid yeast will bring a batch up to about 5 percent ABV, so you might have to buy two or learn how to make your own yeast starter. That means activating the yeast before brewing and coaxing it into reproducing enough for you use the way you want to. Of course, the bonus is that if you have the knowledge, you can keep the yeast

starter going and not have to buy new yeast when you want to brew again.

GROW YOUR OWN
Granted, you'll need a little outside yeast to get you started. As I just said, though, it's possible for you to create your own little yeast farm and keep the operation in house, as they say. Yeast starters are one way of going about it. Another is to keep the lees – the accumulated yeast and other stuff left as scum in your fermentation vessel.

Professional brewers treat their yeast strains with all the care that they do their real children. Yeasts are a valuable and often guarded treasure. With enough time and creativity, pro brewers can sculpt their yeasts into something truly unique that will set their beers apart from the pack. They will then use those strains over and over until they show signs of weakening.

PRO TIP: I'm sure that you have at least one microbrewery or brew pubs not too far away. Have you ever met the brewer? Are you on friendly terms with him or her? Sometimes a professional brewer is willing to share a small amount of their treasured yeast – if they like someone and if they know it's purely for home brewing instead of for sale or sharing with other people – if you ask nicely enough. You may even get some great stories about how they started brewing and mistakes or triumphs they experienced along the way. The worst that can happen is that they say no. Well, that's not true. I suppose they could say, "Get out of my pub and never come back." Maybe you should put one of your local pubs on a "do not ask" list, just to make sure you still have somewhere to kick back and enjoy good beer.

MAKING A STARTER
A starter is really nothing more then a mini beer brewed ahead of time to give the yeast a head start. You can do it with dried yeasts but it's almost a requirement with liquid yeast do to the limited amount that comes in one of those tubes. Also when

doing this remember to use all the same sterilization techniques you would when actually brewing your beer.

Bring 2 cups of water to a boil and add ½ cup of DME (Dried Malt Extract). Boil for 10 minutes while stiring. Place pan in ice water bath until the temperature falls to around 70 degrees or whatever temp your yeast packet recommends. Once it's down to the right temp then mix in your yeast and pour the whole lot into a container that it can sit in for a while. Some people just use a large glass measuring cup. Others use large beer bottles, like a growler. Me, I like to use an Erlenmeyer Flask. It adds to that whole mad scientist vibe I'm going for.

Now whatever you do DO NOT put an airlock on it. You want it to breathe. Remember, air makes yeast grow. So cover it loosely in aluminum foil.

Now you will want to make your starter no less then 30 minutes before you need it. I recommend actually doing it at least a day or two beforehand. Me? I make my starters on Monday or Tuesday for the next Saturday's cook. Also I use wonderful tool called a Stir Plate.

A stir plate, pictured above (under the flask), is a little box with a spinning magnet in it that spins a second magnet, called a stir bar, that is placed in your starter. There are a couple reasons to do this. It oxygenates the mixture and really promotes the growth of your yeast. It keeps the yeast mixed up and in good contact with all the nutrients. And best of all, it looks like a little cyclone in a bottle, once again adding to the mad scientist vibe!

Stir plates normally start at around $75 but there is another solution, you can make one with less then $20 in parts from Radio Shack if you are really into the whole DIY thing.

Tools for the Job

I like to think that anyone can brew at home, and for the most part, that's true. Anyone with a little extra spending cash can take a shopping list to the store or pick out a (quality, but more on that later) home-brewing kit. Before even that necessary step happens, though, I find that many potential brewers overlook the most basic of tools they'll need to make their own beer: a place to brew and a place to store it. In other words, if you cook only off a Bunsen burner or in the microwave, or if you live in a studio apartment where you can't even swing a cat, you might be better off buying a six pack at the corner store, at least for the time being. Trust me, brewing tends to expand into the space allotted to it and then a bit more.

The place to do your brewing needs to include a stove/range or some sort of heating element. I like to cook outdoor and I use a burner and propane setup. You will need access to water as a decent amount of counter-top or other flat workspace. Try to make it comfortable, but also know that both processes can be messy. You are making sugar water and it will adhere to everything. Don't try it on top of Grandma's heirloom area rug, you have been warned.

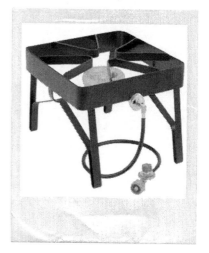

The place to store the brew needs to be a low traffic place where it can sit and be kept at the right temperature for long

periods of time. For ales, this is room temp. For lagers and more specialty brews, this could require an extra refrigerator or even a chest freezer (turn the temp turned way up). Take that into account before choosing your beer recipe. I like to use an infrared thermometer to check ambient temps in the area. They cost $20 to $30 and you will find all sorts of uses for them.

Only then should you move on to your shopping list. To start with, let's assume that you're a new brewer who is planning on brewing mostly from malt extracts (as 70-80 percent of home brewers do) and brewing in 5-gallon batches. Here are the basics of what you'll need:

4 to 6-gallon stockpot of stainless steel or enamel with a lid. This will be the boiler, in which you'll combine malt and water to make your wort.

6-gallon food-grade plastic fermenting container that has a lid and can accept an airlock (or similar sized glass carboy). Most brews are based on 5 gallons but you need the extra space for the head or foam that will form while it ferments.

Note: The carboy is far and away the favorite among serious brewers. It's also a pain in the ass to clean, easily broken, hard to move and expensive. Your carboy should come with an air lock/fermentation lock and the matching rubber stopper. If not, you'll have to buy those separate.

PRO TIP: Anything glass used in the brewing process should be tinted, usually brown, because light can affect fermentation. If for some reason you have clear glass, use an old T-shirt or a dark trash bag to cover your container and keep all light out. 10-gallon plastic bucket or cooler (I like the kind with the spigot on the bottom). This container will hold our brew for a short time when we're transferring it.

5 to 10 feet of clear plastic tubing, about 3/8 or 1/2 inch in diameter and an Auto Siphon. This will be used to siphon the brew between fermentations and into your bottles.

Bottle caps and a bottle capper. Neither is expensive, and a quality capper will last you for years to come.

About 48 12-ounce beer bottles (non-screw top only) or 24 22-ounce bottles. The best 22-ounce bottles are often champagne bottles. Just make sure the bottle will accept your caps.

PRO TIP: Buy, drink and keep bottles of Grolsh beer. Their re-sealable caps make capping so much easier, and the rubber stoppers on those caps can be replaced as needed.

A bottling tip (or a funnel, though it's more difficult) to help fill the bottles.

A hydrometer. The most scientific tool at your disposal, a hydrometer is used to measure the "specific gravity" or density of a liquid. Water, for example, will measure a flat 1.000. When you dissolve sugar (or malt or hops) into the water, that reading will rise. You'll use those readings to gauge the sugar

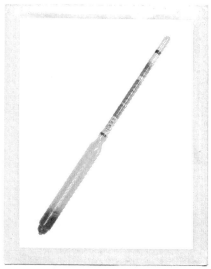

level and therefore where the brew is along the fermentation process. You can also estimate ABV with the hydrometer.

Thermometer with a range from freezing (32 degrees) up to 212 degrees.

Scale that measures up to at least 16 ounces.

A glass measuring cup that can hold up to 16 ounces or more. This is for dissolving and activating the yeast.

A spoon you can sterilize. Do not use a wooden spoon. Stainless steel is the best option.

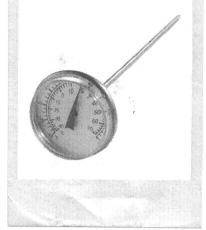

Sanitizing products and tools (such as brushes, sponges and spray bottles). See the next chapter.

If you're using anything other than pure extracts, a strainer.

A brewing notebook or journal. I like to use a tablet running a custom spreadsheet.

Again, this is a basic list of the bare necessities. If you take up all-grain brewing, the list grows a lot longer and more expensive. Plus, every brewing catalog is full of nifty little devices and tools that make things faster or easier. While tempting they are not necessary, especially when you're starting out. Try to keep your budget low until you know how much you're going to like (or love? Or come to hate?) this new hobby. If it still seems like a lot of money, remember the cost will be repaid over hopefully lots and lots of batches of your own brew.

Which brings me to the subject of home-brewing kits. These are not all bad news and some can be quite good. I'm a big fan of modern man making brewing easier, and this is one way he has. The best brew kits are sold at specialty home-brew stores, and for less than $100, you can get everything on my list except the bottles.

Less reputable are the cheap-ass kits you can buy at Wal-Mart or Bed, Bath, Beyond. I do not recommend brewing equipment sold within a few feet of underwear or shower curtains, but use your own best judgment and the list above to see if they can cut muster.

I will say this, if you are buying pieces then Wal-Mart can be your friend. I have found the same or similar items that a local brew shop sells at Wallyworld for half price or less. It seems when you attach the words "Home Brewing" to anything there is an immediate price bump.

Buying a pre-assembled kit can make sense for a novice brewer, if that kit is purchased for the equipment. When the equipment also comes with the beer ingredients – malt and hops extract – and its own instructions, you have to be very careful.

Off the top, how fresh are those ingredients? You have absolutely no idea, unless you can have a conversation with the person who assembled the kit. Those ingredients may also be skimpy. I've heard of kits that contain 1 can of malt extract (about 4 pounds) instead of the recommended 5-6 pounds of extract for a 5-gallon batch. Some kits' instructions even insist that you don't need to boil the wort? You're often better off getting your ingredients and instructions from a more trusted source.

And one last thing about equipment, I want to revisit that Carboy vs. Fermenter statement from above. You really have three main options, Glass Carboy, Plastic Carboy and Plastic pail style fermenter. Me? I go with the pail.

Hate on me all you like but they are easier to clean, they are easier to move and I have never once snapped a neck off of one or had the whole thing shatter on me as I have had happen with a glass carboy. Do they look as pretty? No. Do they work? Yes. They are cheap, efficient and they get the job done. As opposed to glass which is heavy, hard to clean and when it breaks you get to pull a large chunk of glass out of your leg. Fun times!

Cleanliness Before Possible Drunkeness

Look, I know it's not glamorous. I know it's not fun. In fact, cleaning and sanitizing your brewing equipment is often called the janitorial side of home brewing, and while we all might dream of one day growing up to be a real brewer, no one fantasizes about a career as a janitor. Sadly, there's just no way around sanitization. Look at it this way. Take the 15 minutes time to make sure everything is sanitized properly or risk wasting hours and hours of hard work and money on a batch that goes bad because you were lazy.

Fermenting is the process of making food for yeast, a single-celled fungus, but it's not like yeast's tastes are so unique. You're intentionally making the perfect environment for all sorts of nasties, bacterial and fungal. It's like opening a donut shop next door to a police station. It will draw them in like magnets, so it's up to you to create a state-of-the-art security system that keeps the cops – um, the unwanted microorganisms out.

For starters, do you know the difference between cleaning and sanitizing? Cleaning is like when you do your regular kitchen dishes. You make sure everything stuck on is scraped off, then you use a dish soap followed by a good rinse and dry. That dish is clean, and you'll clean some of your brewing equipment just like that.

That dish is not sanitized, though. Neither dish soap or warm water or your favorite drying towel remove microorganisms. That takes either high temperatures – like boiling – or disinfecting chemicals like bleach. Actually, a bleach solution of 1 Tablespoon chlorine bleach to 1 gallon of water, in this case. Ten minutes in that solution causes an almost 100 percent kill rate for microorganisms. Of course, that "sanitized" dish is not ready for dinner. It must be thoroughly rinsed after being soaked in the solution in order to make it safe for contact with anything you're going to put in your body.

Sanitation is key from the very beginning to the very end of home brewing. Seriously, don't be surprised if you spend more time washing and bleaching and rinsing than you do with the actual brewing. You'll have to wash/sanitize the same tools several times, even. This is the cosmic joke of brewing. In order to enjoy the bubs, you're going to have to do the scrubs. There's no use bitching about it. Build a bridge and get over it, the sooner the better.

PRO TIP: Don't forget your work surfaces when you sanitize before brewing or between steps. A clean tool won't do you any good if you put it down on a dirty counter top.

There are two stages of the brewing process in terms of keeping it clean and germ-free. The first is the hot stage. This begins when you first boil your water (as you're likely to do if you want to remove municipal chlorination) and lasts through all your boiling until you begin to cool down your wort. That stage is different, because boiling kills the bad stuff. You don't want to ever intentionally use an unsanitized tool, of course, but if something slips in the mix, the boiling is your insurance policy.

Once you begin to cool down your wort – specifically to about 140 degrees, the point at which microbes can survive – that insurance expires. This is the cold part of the process. There won't be enough heat ever again to save your butt, so extra vigilance is required.

Did you take a reading with your thermometer or hydrometer? That needs to be sanitized before you take a reading again. Did you stir with a spoon? That spoon cannot be used to stir again, unless you re-sanitize. Ditto for tubing, and doubly so for bottles, which are the biggest pain and biggest liability in the whole procedure. To be honest, I hate bottles and won't use them. I prefer to bottle in larger bottles like growlers or keg. But that is a more advanced discussion for another time.

Whatever you are cleaning, especially if it is plastic, you'll need to use the softest possible tool that will still get the job done. If you're using stainless steel, go ahead and reach for those green Scotchbrite pads that scrub so well. If you have plastic, use a softer sponge or you risk creating even tiny scratches where microbes can grow in the future. You can avoid plastic with most tools if you try, but that's not possible with your tubing, so treat it with care and replace it often. It's not like it's a pricey item.

PRO TIP: Examine all of your tools, top to bottom in search of hard to reach places and blind spots. Your spoon might have small ridges or valleys in the handle for decoration, for instance. Find all the corners of your carboy and find out how to make sure every millimeter of your air lock is germ free.

Back to the bottles, what kind do you plan on using? The majority of new brewers tend to save their empties from store-bought beers, which is cool as long as the original caps weren't screw-off tops.

The first time you prepare these is going to be the worst. If possible, you're going to want to clean them out ASAP after you finish the original beer. The dregs of yeast will harden like the cholesterol in your arteries otherwise and is as hard to remove as plaque from your teeth. Soak the bottle to loosen the label and completely remove it and the glue residue left behind. The wet paper and stickiness would otherwise be calling out to microbes, saying, "Make your home here!" Soak the bottles in the bleach solution for several hours or preferably overnight. Then, of course, they're going to need a really good rinse before bottling your beer. After you rinse the bottles, they need to be kept completely sterile until you fill them, so try to do that as close to bottling time as you can. Also, never use dish soap on your bottles unless it's been thoroughly rinsed, then bleached and rinsed again. Any trace of soap can seriously mess with the head you'll get on the finished brew.

PRO TIP: How can you tell if your carboy or your bottles are completely clean AND sterile? After rinsing off the bleach, spray the inside with some very hot water. The water will steam up inside the glass and condense along the walls. If you see patterns in the condensation, there is still scum that needs to be removed.

You can also buy new bottles, of course. Those still need to soak overnight and go through the rest of the steps, though. As for the bottle caps, I boil those suckers and then let them sit in the boiled water until the exact moment I'm ready to use them. The flat discs are just too easy to contaminate otherwise.

Not all contamination comes from your tools, though. Sometimes it's about how you handle your batch, for example, siphoning. We've all seen it on TV and many have done it ourselves, getting a siphon started by putting our mouth on the hose and sucking until the liquid starts flowing. Do you trust how clean your mouth is? I don't, if even just for my foul language. It's a risk and lets face it, no one else wants to drink from a bottle filled this way.

You can choose to do it cleaner by filling the hose with cold, clean, boiled water, then putting that hose in the brew. The liquid will start flowing through the tube as the water – put that in a waste container – then you shift the hose over to your fermenting vessel when you start to see the beer. It's extra work, yes, but it does offer a better guarantee. Also, when you're transferring your beer from one container to another, try not to splash it around. Every little bit it's exposed to air is another chance for it to pick up a bug. Be gentle. Also stir gently for the same reason.

Follow the rules, do your time cleaning, and there's no reason you can't make a good clean batch your first time and every other time afterward. Still, it happens. How do you tell if your batch has been contaminated? Contamination can cause over-carbonation, sour aromas or flavors, cloudiness and even moldy beer. That mold isn't overly harmful, meaning that it won't make you sick, but it does ruin your beer. One surefire sign of contamination is a ring around the inside of the bottle just at the level of the liquid inside. Sorry, that's a goner.

Your First Batch

All the build up and all that reading, and I'm guessing that all you really wanted to do was get out of that chair and start brewing. Your patience is rewarded and your time has finally arrived, my friend, though I have one last request before you begin: Read all the way through the instructions and, indeed, all the way to the end of this book before you actually set things in motion, including choosing a recipe and buying ingredients. Mother Nature is magical, but you also can't rush her if you want great results. Just ask Dr. Frankenstein.

These instructions are geared toward novices using malt extracts or extracts with the addition of some whole grains. They're not for all-grain beers (sorry, next book). I've tried to make these steps as easy to read as possible so when you do brew, you can check off each step as you go along and be less likely to forget anything. FYI, the making of the wort and the syphoning are often the hardest step for beginners. Prepare, be careful and don't cuss at yourself too much if you, like so many others, have a hard time in those steps. Also, consider the purchase of an auto-syphon. They can make a hard job much easier.

PRO TIP: Photocopy or print out a copy of the steps and physically check steps off, make notes about observations or changes in the margin. Transfer those notes to your brewing journal later. That paper can get messy and stained during brewing while your brewing journal stays clean.

PREPARATION
Boil your water the day before. If possible, keep it cold in the fridge. You should have a gallon or two on top of the 5 gallons

you'll use in the recipe. Store in an open container to allow the water to breathe.

Have all the tools you'll need sanitized and ready to go. Put on an apron if you have one! Remember, this can get sticky!
To make your malt extract easier to pour, fill your sink with hot water and let it sit there for until warm.

Prepare your grains. If they are not already cracked then you can crush them with a rolling pin (or pulse in a food processor, just enough to open the grain) and put them in cheesecloth or a mesh bag.

Add your hops to smaller mesh bags.
MAKING THE WORT
Bring half of the water to a boil and then transfer to a sterilized cooler, the kind with a tap at the bottom. Place on a counter for easy access later. Then place the other half of the water in the pot and start to bring it to a boil. Make sure to leave enough empty space in the pot to allow for the wort to foam.

While that is heating up add your bag of grains and bring the heat up to 150 to 158 degrees and then turn off the heat and allow the grains to steep for 10 to 20 minutes (Heat and time may vary according to recipe). Remove the grains from the pot with a large spoon and while holding it over the pot pour 4 cups or so of hot water from the cooler over the bag to wash the grains. Carefully squeeze the bag to get all the water out.

Discard grains (or use them for fertilizer) and bring the pot to a hard boil. Add your warmed malt extract slowly, stirring all the while. We don't want any clumps of syrup to remain. It should totally dissolve.

PRO TIP: If you have a can of malt extract, after you pour it in, fill the can with hot, clean water to pick up the last of the extract, then pour that into the pot, as well.

BOILING
Bring the pot back to a rolling boil, which means it will continue to boil even if you're stirring it. You can cover the boiler to make it boil faster, but still pay attention.

Foam is normal, but if it's going to overflow, stirring or spraying the foam with water will help calm it down.

Add your hops extract and/or boiling hops as your recipe dictates.

Boil for the time recommended by your recipe. An average for extract beers is about 45 minutes in my experience, but your recipe might be different.

COOLING
The boiling hot water is too hot for our yeast, so it needs to chill down to at least 78 degrees or as low as 70 degrees.

Put the wort (with the lid on) in a large sink or even bathtub filled with cold water. The pot will heat up that water, and you can drain and refill with more cold water as many times as you need. It will take a long time to get it down to temp. DO NOT add ice to your wort. It's likely not sanitary and will cool too fast.
Meanwhile, activate your yeast. In your sanitized measuring cup, mix your yeast with water that's about 95-105 degrees. Cover the cup, and let it sit 10 minutes. It should foam up a bit.

PRO TIP: Consider investing or even building a wort chiller. There are several styles but the most common is a copper coil that snakes in and then back out. You connect a water hose to this to cool it down and then immerse it in your wort. Make sure to do so about 15 minutes before you stop boiling your wort so as to sanitize it.

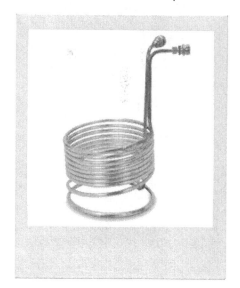

FERMENTATION
If you have sediment or remaining whole grains, you'll want to strain those out now.

Add the yeast, stirring all the while. We want oxygen to interact with the yeast at this point to get the ball rolling. Stir for a solid five minutes.

Put the liquid in your fermenter. Add your reserved cool boiled water to bring the volume up to 5 gallons. If you can, pick up the fermenter and shake it a bit to combine the warm and cool waters. Careful, it's going to be HEAVY

Attach your air lock/fermentation lock.

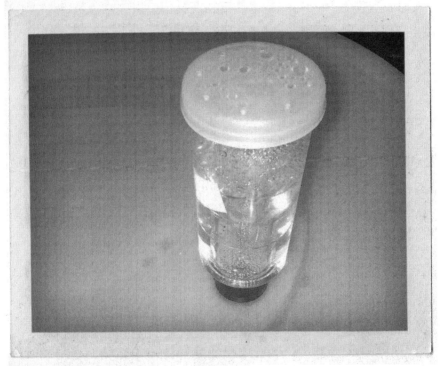

Put your fermenter somewhere quiet, dim and at room temperature. It's best if it's placed on a piece of cardboard or a towel. The lock will bubble a bit.
Let it ferment for a few days (3-5, generally). Your recipe will let you know about how long, and your hydrometer readings will level off when this stage of fermentation is complete.

PRIMING AND BOTTLING

Place your fermenter on a waist-high counter top or higher, and put your secondary container (sterile!) on the floor below. Use your tubing to siphon the beer from the carboy down to the container. Keep the tubing above the level of the sediment at the bottom of the fermenting vessel. That's normal. The yeast cells have died and fallen out of the suspension. Remember, fill the tubing with clean water, clamp it, add it to the beer, and unclamp it for the most sanitary way of starting the siphon. Have another container to catch the water, then switch containers for the beer. Try not to splash. Be gentle. We don't want a lot of oxygen introduced.

Prepare your priming liquid (extra sugar molecules to kick off another round of fermentation). This will be either 3/4 cup of corn sugar or 1 1/4 cups dried malt extract, which you will combine with 16 ounces (1 pint) of boiling water. Stir gently for about 2-3 minutes. Stir this (again, gently) into the beer.

Create another siphon and fill your (sterile!) bottles using the bottling tip, or the funnel if you're going to old-fashioned route. Cap your bottles with your bottle capper.

STORAGE

Place your bottles upright in a quiet, dim spot at room temperature or just a little colder. Secondary fermentation is taking place in the bottle, so too cold will halt the process. Too warm will sour your beer.

Leave them for about two weeks to allow carbonization to occur as the secondary fermenting continues.
If desired or if your recipe recommends it, you can further condition your beer for another week or two in fridge, which can improve the flavor.

DRINKING

A small layer of dead yeast sediment is normal. Pour your home brew slowly with your glass at an angle to preserve the carbonization. Leave as much sediment as you can in the bottom of the bottle, though a little bit won't hurt anyone or anything.

Cheers! Enjoy your home-brewed beer. Share it with friends and family. Or hey, hoard it for yourself. It's your beer to do with what you choose.

When you're done, though, wash out that bottle right away to make your job that much easier when you brew next time.

Again, these are pretty basic instructions for a brewer using only or mostly extracts. Some recipes will vary in exact temperatures or time measurements. Once you get used to the process, you'll better understand which parts are fluid and which are not.

Remember to write down everything in your journal! You learn something new every brew.

PRO TIP: If you decide to tweak a recipe or attempt to improve upon a recipe, change only one thing at a time and document it well. If you change two or three or more ingredients or methods, you won't be able to tell what caused the differences in the resulting beer.

NOTES: I'm often asked how much water to use. Remember water is the vehicle, not an ingredient. You just need to start with enough water to cook the ingredients that you are adding. Usually for a 5 gallon batch that would be no less then 2 gallons to start with. But you want to keep an eye on what you are cooking. Lots of grains absorb water. In fact they can absorb a LOT of water. Also as it boils water evaporates, so your wort and get thick very easily. If that happens you may need to add more water to thin it out. It should be like a very thin soup in consistency.

Be careful about starting out with too much water. To much and it can boil over. You won't have room for the foam that will happen when you add the malt. You can always add more but you can't really take any away.

Then when it comes time to put it in the fermenter you can just top off what ever you have to bring it up to 5 gallons. It's important at this point to have that much as there needs to be a correct sugar to water ratio for the yeast to do their magic.

And lest you forget, always use sanitized water. That is water that has been prepped and boiled and stored in a sanitized container. Also DO NOT add hot water at this point as you could raise the temp to a point where it will kill the yeast.

The Many Faces of Beer

The main defining characteristic of beers is ales versus lagers, but there are a lot – a LOT – of variations inside both of those categories. Whether you're a craft-beer drinker or not, you've likely not tried every variety under the sun. In other words, maybe you haven't found your ultimate favorite yet!

Here's a very basic rundown of what the world offers in terms of types of beers so you can decide which varieties you want to brew in your own home.

ALES:
BELGIAN ALES
This country played a big part in beer history and its styles have shaped much of what we consider modern brewing tradition. There are several subcategories of Belgian ale, including:

Abbey Beers. Originally, these beers were called abbey ales because they were brewed at or distributed through a religious abbey. They're divided into Single (blondes), Dubbel (malty and darker), Tripel (the most popular with light color but high ABV, usually over 8 percent) and Quadrupel (the darkest and strongest).
Belgian Browns. Combines malt sweetness with a signature sourness, usually served unfiltered.

Golden/Blonde. Ranging from a middle-range alcohol content to deceptively high (9 percent), these are fruity and aromatic.

Lambics. This Belgian style uses the oldest method of brewing beer, spontaneous cultivation, which gives them an exotic sour tinge, and some can take up to three years to fully ferment. Subcategories include Fruit (added during maturation), Gueuze (similar to champagne) and Straight (rare, with very little carbonation, usually tapped from cask).

Red Beers. As the name suggests, these beers are red and are also sharp and acidic. They differ from brown beers because they're usually filtered.

Saison. These are summer beers designed to quench your thirst, though they're now made year-round. Often dry, they're colored amber or orange and are heavily hopped and spiced. Seasonal herbs and flavors are often added.

Trappist Beers. Trappists are a very strict order of monks, and there are only seven official Trappist breweries, six in Belgium and one in the Netherlands. They re-ferment in the bottle to make a strong ale, usually with a slight rum flavor from sugar added in the brewing process.

Wit Bier. These beers are spiced with coriander and dried orange peels and are made up of malted barley and raw wheat. They're thought of as similar to all-wheat beers but are easier to filter.

GERMAN ALES
The birthplace of lagering, German still has a deep tradition of ale brewing. Its popular styles include:

Alt Bier: A copper ale of all barley fermented with a single yeast cell.

Beliner Weisse: A light wheat beer with low alcohol content (3-3.5 percent) famous for its tartness.

Dunkel Weizen: This beer translates as "dark wheat" and has clove and banana aromas and a caramel flavor.

Hefe-weizen. This beer is classically unfiltered and offers aromas of banana and clove. They're also sometimes called Weiss beers (white) because of the color and head.

BRITISH ALES
As a former British colony, American beer tradition borrows a great deal from that of Britain, which includes England, Ireland, Scotland and Wales. Styles include:

Barley Wine (English/Scottish). Treated with utmost respect, this brew has richness and depth and an ABV similar to wine. Also like wine, they're allowed to age for significant periods of time.

Bitters. These are the showpieces of British hops. They range from gold to copper in color, and include Ordinary (light, sometimes called cream ale when tapped with nitrogen), Special Bitter (robust and dry) and Extra Special Bitters (ESB, richest in malt and hops).

English Browns. A medium-body ale with mid-range maltiness and little hop flavor. Also called nut-brown ale and often unfiltered.

India Pale Ale (IPA). Extra hops and a high alcohol content (up to 8 percent) kept this beer from spoiling when shipping it to troops all over the British Empire. There are also Imperial IPAs, which bring the already strong hops to another level. Pale Ales. Actually golden to copper in color, these are called pale to tell them apart from Porters and Stouts. Low maltiness and a spotlight on English hops give them an assertive flavor for a lighter beer.

Porters. Of medium darkness, Porters are full-bodied and slightly cloudy.

Scottish Ales. Malty caramel in flavor, these range from amber to brown in color. Subcategories include Light (thinner in body, low bitterness), Heavy (stronger in flavor) and Scotch Ale, which is Scottish ales big brother (high in alcohol and intensely full bodied, sometimes smoky or peaty).

Stouts. There are five major types of this darkest, black ale: Irish Dry (dry roasted, excellent head), Sweet/Cream (with milk sugars and low hopping), Oatmeal (caramel and chocolate in flavor), Imperial (boldest and strongest) and Foreign-Style (still low hopping with higher alcohol content). Strong Ales. Amber to brown, these are also called Old Ales because of the longer aging process that makes them smooth. They can also be as high as 11 percent ABV.

AMERICAN ALE
American Pale Ale is very recent, only developed about 1980, and it notably uses American hops, which gives it a higher hops profile than the British Pale Ale. It's lighter in color than an amber ale and not as hoppy as an IPA.

LAGERS:
BOCK
Strong beers that were originally top-fermented, this lager made mostly of wheat was the main beer to spread the process of lagering throughout the world. They're often dark and slightly high in ABV, averaging about 6.5 percent. Types include, Helles Bock. The lightest in color with a noble hop aroma but low bitterness. Doppelbocks. Uses more barley as its base and has a sweet finish. Traditional Bock. A few steps darker than Helles in color and with even less bitterness without a higher ABV.

DUNKEL
These dark (the meaning of the word Dunkel) lagers are linked to Bavaria, though they're made in other regions of Germany, too. It's malty with only gentle hopping and an ABV of 4.5-6 percent.

PILSENERS
This now super-popular type of beer began in the Czech Republic in the town of Pilsen. It's set apart by its golden color and the use of Saaz hops. They're about 5 percent ABV on average. The German versions of pilsners have a stronger hop bitterness, though the Bohemian Pilsners are sweeter, full-bodied and use the original Saaz.

OKTOBERFEST
Around 6 percent alcohol, this brew was originally called March Beer (Ur-Marzen) because that's the month it was made. Its popularity happened to blow up just as Munich held its first Oktoberfest celebration, and the name stuck. They're full-bodied with low to moderate bitterness and an amber color.

Recipes

At this point, admit it. You're an expert! You know so much more about beer than you learned in years or even decades of drinking the stuff. In terms of the actual brewing process, though, you need to remember that you're still a novice.

Therefore, we're only going to cover some introductory recipes here and only those recipes using malt extracts. We will throw in some fun stuff in the way of boiling and finishing hops, sugars and such, but save the real experimentation for later, when you've mastered the basics. Walk before you run.

Unless the recipe says otherwise, use the step-by-step brewing instructions found in the Your First Batch chapter. All recipes will yield about 5 gallons.

FOUNDATIONAL ALE RECIPE

6 pounds canned, pre-hopped light malt syrup
1 ounce hop pellets (choose your flavor)
2 packets ale yeast
3/4 cup liquid corn syrup (or 4 ounces dry corn syrup)

1.   Boil 1.5 gallons of your clean water. Remove from heat and stir in malt syrup until it dissolves.
2.   Bring the pot back to a boil, and continue to boil for 50 minutes, stirring frequently.
3.   Stir in hops pellets. Cook for 20 minutes.
4.   Put 3.5 gallons of clean, cold water in your carboy. Siphon your wort into your carboy. Top up to make 5 gallons if necessary.
5.   Create yeast starter. Bring 1 cup of clean water up to a temperature of 95-105 degrees. Add the yeast, stir gently and cover for 10 minutes.
6.   When temperature of wort mixture is below 75 degrees, add your yeast starter. Put on fermentation lock.
7.   In about 14 days when primary fermentation is complete – your hydrometer will register the same level two days in a row – add 3/4 cup corn syrup dissolved in hot water. Bottle your beer.
8.   Age at least 2 weeks and up to 8 weeks.

INDIA PALE ALE (IPA)

7 pounds amber malt extract, liquid or dried
2/3 cup dried malt extract for priming
2 ounces Northern Brewer pellets for boiling hops, 14-20 (divided)
2 packages top-fermenting yeast
1 teaspoon Irish Moss (for clarification)
1 ounce Cascade hops pellets for finishing hops

1.   Boil 2 gallons of water, turn off heat and add malts.
2.   Boil for 20 minutes, then add 1 ounce (half) of the Northern Brewer boiling hops.
3.   Boil for another 20 minutes. Add remaining 1 ounce of boiling hops and Irish Moss.
4.   Boil another 20 minutes. Turn off the heat.
5.   Put 3 gallons of clean, cold water in your carboy. Siphon your wort into your carboy. Top up to make 5 gallons if necessary.
6.   Create yeast starter. Bring 1 cup of clean water up to a temperature of 95-105 degrees. Add the yeast, stir gently and cover for 10 minutes.
7.   When temperature of wort mixture is below 75 degrees, add your yeast starter. Put on fermentation lock.
8.   When primary fermentation is complete – your hydrometer will register the same level two days in a row – bottle your beer.
9.   Age 3-5 weeks.

BLONDE ALE
1/2 pound Crystal malt (for steeping)
1/2 pound CaraPils malt
6 pounds Extra Light Dry Malt Extract
1.75 ounces Willamette pelletized hops (divided)
1 teaspoon Irish Moss (for clarification)
2 packages top-fermenting yeast

1.   Bring 3 gallons of clean water to 150 F. Put steeping grains in bag and steep for 1 hour. Lift bag out, squeeze of extra liquid and throw away.
2.   Bring water to boil. Remove from heat and stir in 3 pounds of malt extract. Boil for another 40 minutes.
3.   Add 3/4 ounce of your hops and your Irish Moss. Return to a boil. Boil for 15 minutes.
4.   Add 3/4 ounce of your hops and all of your remaining malt extract. Return to a boil for 5 minutes.
5.   Add final 1/4 ounce of hops. Boil for 5 minutes.
6.   Put 2 gallons of clean, cold water in your carboy. Siphon your wort into your carboy. Top up to make 5 gallons if necessary.
7.   Create yeast starter. Bring 1 cup of clean water up to a temperature of 95-105 degrees. Add the yeast, stir gently and cover for 10 minutes.
8.   When temperature of wort mixture is below 75 degrees, add your yeast starter. Put on fermentation lock.
9.   In about 7 days when primary fermentation is complete – your hydrometer will register the same level two days in a row – bottle your beer.
10. Age at least 2 weeks.

BROWN ALE

4 pounds malt extract syrup
6 ounces crystal malt
1.5 ounces black malt
2 ounces roasted barley
1 ounce flaked or rolled barley
1 ounce wheat malt
2 ounces Northern Brewer hops
1 ounce Goldings hops
2/3 cup dark brown sugar
2 packages top-fermenting yeast

1.   Boil 1.5 gallons of your clean water. Remove from heat and stir in malt syrup until it dissolves.
2.   Put other grains and your hops in a mesh bag or cheesecloth (otherwise you can opt to strain them out later) and add to the pot. Bring the pot back to a boil, and continue to boil for 60 minutes, stirring frequently.
3.   Put 3.5 gallons of clean, cold water in your carboy. Siphon your wort into your carboy. Top up to make 5 gallons if necessary.
4.   Create yeast starter. Bring 1 cup of clean water up to a temperature of 95-105 degrees. Add the yeast, stir gently and cover for 10 minutes.
5.   When the temperature of wort mixture is below 75 degrees, add your yeast starter. Put on fermentation lock.
6.   In about 10 days when primary fermentation is complete – your hydrometer will register the same level two days in a row – add the brown sugar dissolved in hot water. Bottle your beer.
7.   Age at least 2 weeks.

PORTER

6.5 pounds liquid light malt extract
1 pound liquid Munich malt extract
1 pound Crystal 40L malt, crushed
3/4 pound Chocolate malt, crushed
1/2 pound Black patent malt, crushed
2 ounces Cascade hops
2 packages top-fermenting yeast

1.   Bring 3 gallons of clean water to 170 F. Put Crystal Malt, Chocolate Malt and Black Patent Malt in a mesh bag and steep for 1 hour. Lift bag out, squeeze of extra liquid and throw away.
2.   Bring water to boil. Remove from heat and stir in malt extract. Return to a boil. Add 1 ounce Cascade hops in a mesh bag and boil for 45 minutes.
3.   Add another 1 ounce Cascade in a mesh bag. Return to a boil for 15 minutes.
4.   Allow to cool. Remove mesh bags.
5.   Put 2 gallons of clean, cold water in your carboy. Siphon your wort into your carboy. Top up to make 5 gallons if necessary.
6.   Create yeast starter. Bring 1 cup of clean water up to a temperature of 95-105 degrees. Add the yeast, stir gently and cover for 10 minutes.
7.   When the temperature of wort mixture is below 75 degrees, add your yeast starter. Put on fermentation lock.
8.   In about 20 days when primary fermentation is complete – your hydrometer will register the same level two days in a row – bottle your beer.

IMPERIAL STOUT

10 pounds Dark dry malt extract
1 pound Cane sugar
1/3 pounds Molasses
12 ounces Crystal Malt
10 ounces Chocolate Malt
3 ounces Roasted Barley
3 ounces Black Patent
2.5 ounces Target Hops (for boiling)
1.5 ounces Target Hops (for finishing)

1.   Bring 2 gallons of clean water to 150 F. Put steeping grains in bag and steep for 3 minutes.
2.   Bring water to boil. Remove from heat and stir malt extract, cane sugar, and molasses. Stir in boiling hops. Boil for 45 minutes.
3.   Add your flavoring hops and boil an additional 15 minutes.
4.   Put 2 gallons of clean, cold water in your carboy. Siphon your wort into your carboy. Top up to make 5 gallons if necessary.

Final Words

Like beer, we humans are made mostly of water. We're just big liquid beasts held up by our skeletons, which are quite handy that way. Instead of creating the biggest and most in-depth manual about home brewing in the world, let this book be a skeleton of knowledge for you in your new hobby of brewing. It should give you the straight-talking, strong foundation on which you can build whatever you want, as high as you want.

You have started your journey but you there is much more to learn. Brewing, distilling, wine and even mead. Come join us on Facebook and be part of the conversation. Brewing is more then a hobby, it's a community and now you are one of us.

So from my house to yours, I raise my glass to you. Cheers!

Questions, Comments, and Thanks

Be sure to visit our blog at www.TheHomeDistiller.com

You can also find us on Facebook at
http://www.facebook.com/TheHomeDistiller.

On the blog you can post questions and comments, find links to materials and tools, and in the future I also hope to be adding additional content such as videos and advanced techniques as well as an FAQ section. See you there!

All equipment mentioned here can be purchased online at our shop, http://www.MoonshiningSupplies.com

For all other inquiries please send an email to:
info@FOIPub.com   Please note that I can not answer technical questions at this email address. Please post those on the blog or Facebook group.

Special thanks to our cover girl. If you would like to submit your picture to be a cover girl on one of our next books, please send an e-mail to girls@thehomedistiller.com.

Extra thanks to Max Johnson, illustrator and photographer extraordinaire. For more of Max's work please check out www.its.max.net

Special Thanks:

This goes out to my home team. To my beautiful wife, Jesse, and my three children:
Duncan, my Big Bear!
Eleanor, a.k.a. Little Miss Princess
and our little bear, Griffin

You are my greatest adventure!

If you liked this book please look for our other books:

How to Make Beer Part II, Advanced Brewing

The Home Distiller's Workbook: Your guide to moonshine

How to Build a Still, a guide from the The Home Distiller.

Red White & Blush; How to taste, serve and buy wine

All of these and more can be found at http://www.FOIPub.com

42713723R00048

Made in the USA
Lexington, KY
03 July 2015